Dating for Introverts

Eliminate Approach Anxiety and Confidently Speak to and Get Dates with the Most Beautiful Women

By

Stuart Killan

© Copyright 2018 Stuart Killan all rights reserved.

The content contained within this book may not be reproduced, duplicated or transmitted without direct written permission from the author or the publisher.

Under no circumstances will any blame or legal responsibility be held against the publisher, or author, for any damages, reparation, or monetary loss due to the information contained within this book. Either directly or indirectly.

Legal Notice:

This book is copyright protected. This book is only for personal use. You cannot amend, distribute, sell, use, quote or paraphrase any part, or the content within this book, without the consent of the author or publisher.

Disclaimer Notice:

Please note the information contained within

this document is for educational and entertainment purposes only. All effort has been executed to present accurate, up to date, and reliable, complete information. No warranties of any kind are declared or implied. Readers acknowledge that the author is not engaging in the rendering of legal, financial, medical or professional advice. The content within this book has been derived from various sources. Please consult a licensed professional before attempting any techniques outlined in this book.

By reading this document, the reader agrees that under no circumstances is the author responsible for any losses, direct or indirect, which are incurred as a result of the use of information contained within this document, including, but not limited to, — errors, omissions, or inaccuracies.

Table Of Contents

Your Free Gift

Introduction

Chapter One: The Setting

    Always Walk Tall

    Approach Her Immediately

    Stop Overthinking

    Use Your Body Language

    Getting Her Number

    How to Deal with External Factors

    What Should You do if a Woman Rejects You?

Chapter Two: How to Start a Conversation

    Find Out What She is Interested in

    Ask Her What She Likes

    Do Not Brag

    Make Your Intentions Clear

What Should You Do if she Rejects Your Advances?

Chapter Three: How to Work on Shyness

Engage Strangers

Have Small Interactions

Make Eye Contact

Embrace Your Shyness

Be Yourself

Practice at Home

Change How You View Rejection

You Cannot Predict the Future

Chapter Four: When Should You Avoid Approaching a Girl

When She Does Not Want to be Bothered

Public Transport

At Work

Conclusion

Your Free Gift

As a way of saying thank you for downloading. I'm offering a free bonus report called *7 Habits of Highly Confident People* that's exclusive to the readers of this book.

Get instant access at http://freeconfidencebook.com

Inside the book you'll discover

- Secrets of The Joker, and why he should be admired
- The one thing confident people *always* do first when confronted with a tough situation – learning this alone can 10X your self esteem
- How to use vision boards to achieve your goals
- Identifying your "hidden talents" – even if you don't think you have any

- The one trait you must MURDER if you are to become successful
- How to never doubt your own abilities again
- Michael Jordan's #1 success secret
- The 4 most dangerous words in your vocabulary (if you're saying these regularly you are killing your own confidence)
- How to succeed as an introvert in an extrovert's world

Download for free at http://freeconfidencebook.com

Introduction

Thank you for purchasing this book, *Shyness: Eliminate Approach Anxiety and Confidently Speak to and Get Dates with the Most Beautiful Women.*

Many men often imagine the worst and do not approach the woman they want to speak to. What they fail to understand is that it is all in their heads. Unless they approach the woman, they are never going to know how she feels.

It is not unusual to be shy when you approach a woman, but that should not stop you from interacting with her. This book will help you understand when to approach a woman, and what you can say to get her attention. It is not difficult to be a nice man, but it is difficult to know exactly what you should do. You must bear in mind that you cannot become confident overnight.

Every chapter of this book will help you understand how you should approach any situation based on the outcome. This is the bridging mindset, where you accept that you are not very confident and slightly anxious and yet you decide to approach a woman.

Over the course of this book, you will learn

when to approach a woman and how to make conversation with her. You will also learn how to take rejection and how you should feel if a woman does not want to speak to you. Do not put yourself down since that will not help you on your journey.

I hope the information in this book eases your anxiety and helps you approach your woman with confidence.

Chapter One: The Setting

It is difficult to approach a woman in public for many reasons. For example, she may want to be alone or she could be waiting for a group of friends. There are some places you should avoid approaching a woman, like the grocery store or the gym, where a woman goes to be by herself.

Most men are worried about approaching a woman in public; however, they are making it harder on themselves by overthinking. This chapter provides some tips on how you can approach a woman in public.

Always Walk Tall

An easy way to approach someone is by displaying outward confidence. To do this, you should approach women by walking tall. Do not slouch when you walk, but stand up straight and approach the woman with your head held high. You can copy icons like Humphrey Bogart and Clint Eastwood when you start off. This approach will show the woman that you are confident, even if you are not too confident about your play. You can practice this walk at home before you head out for your first date.

Approach Her Immediately

Have you ever stood on the sidelines and asked yourself whether the pretty lady across the hall noticed you or not? Well, she did. It is because of this that it is important that you approach a woman immediately in public. When you wait for a long time, you will come off as a 'creep' although you did not mean to. Take a breath, muster up the courage, and walk over to her. At first, it is hard to face rejection, but remember that you are never going to win the lottery if you do not buy a ticket. It is better to approach the woman sooner rather than later. You do not want to be like Alex or Rosie from the book *Where Rainbows End*.

Stop Overthinking

One of the benefits of approaching a woman immediately is that it prevents you from overthinking. You have a specific objective when you approach a woman—strike up a conversation, generate some interest, and make her want to talk to you. If you've ever worked in sales, you know that every email you write must keep the reader hooked. This is the approach you should take when you meet a girl. You do not want her to fall in love with you; you only want her to talk to you. Therefore, keep the conversations light and funny.

Use Your Body Language

When you talk to your friends, you do not face each other fully. However, when you approach a woman it must be from the side, or shift to the side after you have approached her. You should try talking to her over your shoulder and turn in when you want to say something to her. When she wants to speak to you, turn away slightly. This is a natural way to talk to her. Most men speak to a woman as if they are at an interview.

Getting Her Number

When you approach a woman in a place that is not a club or bar, tell her that you want her number because you want to meet her sometime soon. Hand your phone over and ask her to type her number in. Text her something funny like, "This is Adam, the smartest guy you have met all day!"

How to Deal with External Factors

When you approach a girl in public, there are going to be many people who will be observing you, but that should not worry you. Why worry about what others think? If you have made eye contact with the girl you like, walk up to her and speak to her. Do not worry about whether the people in the store will worry that you are a creep. Be confident and approach the girl without worrying about anything.

What Should You do if a Woman Rejects You?

If you are a guy with low confidence, you will tell yourself that you are a loser and no woman in the world will agree to date you. This is a horrible thing to tell yourself. You should remember that there are many women in the world, and there are some who will like you for who you are. Do not approach a woman with overconfidence. You cannot think that a woman will talk to you just because you think you are smart. She must also think you are smart.

If one woman rejects you, all you need to do is wait it out and approach another. You should stop being hard on yourself and stick to the bridging mindset.

Chapter Two: How to Start a Conversation

Most men make the mistake of starting a conversation with a topic that bores women. It is true that some women love sports and politics, but you cannot expect them to be impressed by your opinion on why some people should not play sports. The obvious thing is that you should not bore a girl when you talk to her for the first time. Everybody knows this and yet men sometimes do still bore women. Why do you think that is? The reason is that men often *think* women want to hear something, but that is *not* often what women want to hear.

Find Out What She is Interested in

Some women read *Cosmopolitan* and know what topics interest men most. When you are on a date, a woman may bring up a topic that interests you, but this does not mean that you should drone on and on and bore her to death. Yes, some of the information you share will be interesting, but some of it may want her to jump off a bridge.

Before you delve into long-winded tales, try to find out what your date likes to talk about. An easy way to do this is to just ask her. Based on her expression, you will know if you have the green signal or not.

Ask Her What She Likes

How do you know if a girl is interested in the topics you choose, and how do you handle it if she tells you she is not interested? When she says, "Yes, sometimes," but does not show too much interest, change the topic immediately. But, if she says, "Oh my God, yes! I have been following them my whole life," you have a winner. Take a look at the conversation below:

You: "How often do you travel? Where's the last place you went?"

Her: "I really should travel, but I just can't find the time."

You: "Yeah, it can be hard. What else do you like to do?"

Now that she has told you that travel does not interest her, you cannot tell her about this amazing travel story you had in mind. Since you do not want to bore her, change the question and ask her what other things she likes to do. You must ensure that you frame the question in a way that will make her think. If you simply asked her what she did for fun, she can sound rebellious or cool and tell you that she either works all the time, or does not usually have fun. It is therefore a good idea to ask her a question that will make her sound uncool if she does not have an answer.

So, when you ask her questions like, "What do you do to keep life fun?" she must give you an answer that will make her look cool. These questions ensure that she invests some time in the conversation, and it shows that you want to get to know her better.

Do Not Brag

It is a known fact that women do not like it when men constantly brag about themselves. It is also important to remember that it is a waste of time to try to impress women. Instead, you should make yourself look valuable by trying to increase your worth. The problem here is that you may try too hard, and these actions will seem like you are bragging about your qualities.

It is bad to brag about yourself for the following reasons:

- When she shows some interest in you and you begin to brag, she will think that you are way out of your league. Since she is insecure about herself, she will reject you without thinking twice.

- If she does not desire you, it means she views herself as being more aware and experienced. If you brag about yourself, you strengthen her belief that she is more experienced than you are, and will enjoy watching you go out of your way to impress her.

So, what should you do to increase your value?

Always focus on the fundamentals. Women can see right through your actions. If you did not impress her when you first met her, it will be hard to impress her when you go out on a date. Women are not interested in how you talk about yourself; they are interested in how you conduct yourself.

Make Your Intentions Clear

Women are not only emotional, but are also practical. When a woman is speaking to someone, she asks herself, "Why am I talking to this person?" And if she does not find a good reason, she will excuse herself and leave. If you are approaching women for the first time, you will worry about a woman avoiding conversation by telling you that she must:

- Go back to work
- Find her friends
- Use the restroom
- Go back to class

A woman is not rejecting you when she tells you this. She is unsure of what your motives are. Because of this, you should be direct with her. Let us look at the following conversation.

You: "Hey, is this seat taken?"

Her: "No."

You: "I'm really glad it finally stopped raining!"

Her: "Yeah, me too." (*She is wondering what the point of the conversation is.*)

You: "How's that sandwich?"

Her: "Great."

You: "My favorite thing here is the club sandwich. Ever ordered that before?"

Her: "Yes, I have."

You: "Where do you work that you ended up here for lunch?"

Her: "Sorry, but I have to get back to work. Nice meeting you."

You: "It was great to meet you too."

Did you know what you wanted? Neither did she. It was a weird and awkward conversation, and the girl wanted to get out of there. Most people make this mistake, and they make women wonder why they are having a conversation with them. Women eventually leave because they feel awkward, so ensure that you make your intentions clear. Be direct, open, and honest with her.

What Should You Do if she Rejects Your Advances?

There are some people who are extremely

confident about themselves. They believe that they have so much to say that any woman will be happy to talk to them. Other people are constantly worried about what they will say to a woman if she chooses to talk to them. You should strike a balance in between these mindsets. Tell yourself that there are many topics to choose from, and you can maintain a decent conversation with a woman. You may fail a few times, but once you get the hang of it, you'll know what to say to hold her attention.

Chapter Three: How to Work on Shyness

It is not unusual to be shy, but it makes it difficult for you to approach the woman you have a crush on. From the last two chapters, you know when you should approach a girl and what you should do to strike up a conversation. This chapter gives you some tips that will help you meet the woman of your dreams. When you confront a fear or problem, you will find that you can overcome them with ease.

Engage Strangers

Talk to people at stores. No, you will not come off as a creep for making casual conversation with someone. One of the best ways to overcome shyness is by increasing your comfort with casual conversation. You can approach many people and interact with them in a pressure-free and pleasant environment. This will help you develop confidence. For example, you can approach a customer service associate at any store and ask them for help or for their opinion about a product. The objective is to be polite and brief. You do not want to start a long conversation with people you do not know. You are trying to accustom yourself to talking to strangers.

Have Small Interactions

Once you have the confidence to hold brief conversations with strangers, you can start conversing with people who are not the girl you have a crush on. It is better to start with other people to reduce the pressure or fear of rejection. For example:

- Speak to people when you are at a social gathering or at work, but not to the girl you have a crush on. Practice making conversation.

- If you are at a party, approach someone and ask them where the host purchased the food or drink.

- Approach a colleague or a classmate and try to include some anecdotes when you speak to them. You might tell them about a project you're working on.

When you practice a conversation in a pleasant

environment, you can overcome your fear of rejection. This will help you become more confident when you talk to people.

Make Eye Contact

When you smile and make eye contact, you will seem friendlier and more approachable. Do not constantly look into a person's eyes when you talk to them because that can be unnerving; however, make eye contact occasionally to show them your confidence. It may be difficult at first to smile and look people in the eye. Women find it attractive when you appear friendly. Smiling also helps you feel better about any situation you are in. Numerous studies have shown that smiling makes you feel confident and happier since it releases feel-good chemicals.

Embrace Your Shyness

Regardless of how much you practice, you're going to be shy when you speak to the girl you like. Do not worry about being nervous in front of her. Instead of shying away from the conversation, use your nervousness to begin a conversation with her. You can say something like, "I usually am nervous when I talk to such a beautiful girl." That will stick with her and will make sure she talks to you. Ensure that you use the tips mentioned in the previous chapter about the type of conversation you should have with her.

Be Yourself

People often like to act like somebody they are not. If you are a nice guy, be a nice guy. You do not have to pretend to be a bad boy just to make conversation with the girl you like. You will not come off as being cool or confident when you pretend to be someone else. It is important to remember that you should base any relationship on honesty. If she rejects your advances, swallow your pride and sadness, because you did not pretend to be someone you were not. If it did not work out with the girl you approached, there is certainly someone out there who will like you for you. Be patient.

Practice at Home

To overcome your shyness, practice conversations with people at home. You can stand in front of the mirror and learn to introduce yourself or greet someone with a smile on your face. When you practice regularly, the greeting or introduction becomes muscle memory. This makes it easier for you to greet a stranger since you know what you should say and how you should say it. Ensure that you practice in front of the mirror to see what you look like.

Change How You View Rejection

You are shy because you fear rejection. It is natural for someone to take rejection to heart, but instead of taking it personally, realize that rejection is a learning experience. Rejection often has less to do with you, and more to do with the other person. There are days when women will be in a bad mood or dealing with something terrible. They may also be insecure when they need to deal with others.

It is important to remember that rejection is not the end of the world. If you change your perception, you will learn to embrace rejection. You can learn from the experience and understand how you should interact with other people.

You Cannot Predict the Future

You may often try to predict the future and assess how a situation will turn out before you experience it. Human beings always imagine the worst that can happen to them. This is a way for us to survive. It is difficult to overcome this trait when you are in a situation where you are not in danger. Stop trying to analyze the million things that can go wrong when you approach a girl. Focus instead on how well it can go. You will come off as a confident person.

Chapter Four: When Should You Avoid Approaching a Girl

It is important to know when you should not approach a woman. It is nerve-wracking to approach a woman, but it becomes worse when you approach her when she does not want company. Women all over the world have stories where they were harassed by men who wanted to say hello and invaded their personal space, especially when they wanted to be left alone. If you do the same thing, she will call you a creep and probably walk away.

When She Does Not Want to be Bothered

It is important to remember that men and women communicate differently. The former are taught to directly make their wishes known, while the latter communicate their interests and desires subtly. Women rely on non-verbal communication when they interact with men. If a woman wants to be approached, she may look at you, look away, and look back at you. If she does not want to be approached, she will let you know in the same way!

For example, when a woman does not want you to approach her, she will not make eye contact with you or with anybody in the room. She may stare straight ahead, stare into her phone, look down, zone out, or look anywhere but at one person in the room. These signs mean that she does not want anybody to approach her. She can also use sunglasses or a hoodie to avoid looking at anybody.

If she is wearing earbuds or headphones, you know she does not want you to approach her. She may not be listening to music, but she does not want to be disturbed.

Public Transport

Never approach a woman if she is using public transport. People already wish they were anywhere but on the train, or bus, so it is best to avoid speaking to a woman when she is traveling. All she wants to do is get where she's going as fast as possible, without interacting with people.

If you want to approach the cute girl on the bus, you should be aware that you are approaching someone who is already suffering.

You are not a creep, but she does not know that. She wants to get off the bus without having to deal with another guy who thinks that a woman on the bus has signed up for a speed dating service. Do not speak to a woman who is taking public transport. She has her guard up and does not want to talk to you. If she is interested, she will make the first move.

Remember the signs from the previous section? Keep those in mind when you are using public transport. If a woman is reading or is listening to music, do not speak to her.

At Work

When you approach a woman at work, she will be nice to you because her job demands that of her. You may want to ask the cute barista out on a date, but, remember this—she is often nice to you because you are a customer. Waitresses or bartenders may only nice to you because they want you to tip them. Unfortunately, many people misunderstand these signs, and assume that the woman is into them, so make sure that you do not make the wrong move.

Conclusion

If you are shy, it is difficult to speak to a girl without stuttering or making a fool out of yourself, but do not worry. The fear is only within you. If you build some confidence, you can speak to the girl you have a crush on without stuttering. This fear is present because you are worried about rejection. You are also worried that people will think of you as a failure, but what you should remember is that there are a lot of women out there who will be happy that you went and spoke to them.

I hope the information in this book helps you overcome your fear and helps you speak with confidence to the woman you like. Good luck!